5 *Simple Steps to*
Manage Your Mood

5 Simple Steps to Manage Your Mood

A Guide for Teen Girls:
How to Let Go of Negative Feelings and
Create a Happy Relationship with Yourself
and Others

Book 1 of 3
Words of Wisdom for Teens Series

Jacqui Letran

DUNEDIN, FLORIDA

First edition: © June 1, 2020

This book was previously published as, *5 Simple Steps to Reclaim Your Happiness*!

Table of Contents

Section 1:
Introduction to the
5 Simple Steps to
Manage Your Mood

CHAPTER ONE

5 Simple Steps to Manage Your Mood

Are you frustrated because one bad event can ruin your entire day or maybe even your entire week? Does it seem like no matter what you try to do, you just can't seem to shake those negative thoughts and feelings? Instead of being able to let go of things easily, do you often hang on to things long after everyone else seems to have forgotten about them?

If you answered "yes" to these questions, you are not alone. Many people have a hard time letting things go. Instead, when something goes wrong, they replay that scenario over and over in their head, causing them to feel worse about themselves or worse about the other person, or people involved.

Think about the last argument you had with someone that really bothered you. What was that like? Did you replay the argument over and over and beating yourself up for all the things you wished you had done or said differently? Did you make up conversations that didn't even take place and feeling even more upset? Did you think about other similar situations and spiraling downward into sadness, anger, or pain?

Let's say that after the argument had taken place, you wanted to patch things up. Were you able to shake those negativities so you could do what you wanted to do, or were you weighed down and held back by your mood? Did you feel in control of your mood or did you feel as if your mood was controlling you?

For many people, shaking those negative feelings is difficult even when they want to let things go. This is because they don't understand just how much power and control, they do have over their emotions. Maybe this is where you are right now.

Understanding your feelings and knowing what to do with them may seem like a difficult task right now. However, with the right tools, this task can become manageable and even easy. When you use the 5 simple steps outlined in this book – which are really 5 simple questions – you will understand why you feel the way you do, and what you can to do to let those feelings go. You no longer have to let negative feelings, or a bad mood ruin your day. Instead, you can take charge of your mood and focus on creating a happy relationship with yourself and the people you care about.

The great news is, once you understand how to use these 5 simple questions, you can use them to help you resolve problems with anyone whether it's a parent, a friend, an acquaintance, or even with yourself.

To illustrate how you can use these 5 simple questions, let's look at a scenario that happened between my sixteen-year-old client, Amie, and her mother, Beth.

Beth is at home anxiously waiting for her daughter, Amie, to return. It is 10 p.m., which is thirty minutes past Amie's curfew. Amie is late yet again. Beth continues to watch the clock. Minutes feel like hours. Beth becomes angrier. Beth can't understand why Amie continues to violate her curfew and disrespect her rules.

The fights between Beth and Amie have been escalating these past few months. After their last major argument, Beth grounded Amie for two weeks because Amie returned home three hours late. Amie did her best not to talk to Beth for the entire two weeks. When forced to interact, Amie limited her answers to one or two words. The anger, frustration, and resentment between Beth and Amie continued to grow.

In yet another fight, the following week, Amie screamed at Beth, accusing her of being unreasonable, unfair, and too strict with the curfew. Between sobs, Amie pleaded with Beth to see that she was grown up. Amie asked for some understanding, trust, and respect for her ability to make good decisions for herself.

Like many previous fights, this one ended up with Amie angrily stomping off to her room and slamming her door while Beth stood there feeling frustrated and helpless.

Since the last fight, Beth has been trying to be more lenient when Amie breaks curfew. Instead of yelling at Amie and grounding her, Beth does her best to calmly remind Amie of her curfew. Although Beth felt angry and disrespected inside, outwardly she stays in control and tells Amie, "I am not happy when you come home late. It would be nice if you came home at 10 p.m. I could trust and respect your decisions more that way." Noticing her anger rising, Beth leaves the house and goes for a walk to calm herself down. This happened at least four times in the previous two weeks.

Beth thinks she is handling herself well, but the anger and resentment haven't gone away, in fact, it's been steadily rising. Today, she can no longer contain herself. As the minutes continue to pass, her anger builds. Beth recalls all the times that Amie has violated her trust or in any way acted entitled or ungrateful. Beth becomes livid.

The moment Amie walks in the house, Beth rages at Amie, telling her how she is sick and tired of being disrespected. She adds, "I raised a much better daughter than you. I don't know what I did to deserve this. You are selfish, untrustworthy, and all you do is cause me pain."

Amie stands speechless and confused about what is happening. It's only 10:40 p.m., twenty minutes earlier than previous times when she came home at 11 p.m. to a calm and reasonable mother.

As you can imagine, neither mother nor daughter is happy with the exchange. Both feel angry and disappointed.

Throughout this book, we will examine how Beth and Amie used the 5 simple questions to change their mood by letting go of negative feelings and ultimately create a happier relationship with themselves and with each other.

REMEMBER: While helpful, these 5 questions are not meant to replace professional help. If your situation is difficult to handle, or you don't know how to proceed, please talk to your parents or a trusted adult and ask for help.

---

*"Happiness is not something ready-made.
It comes from your own actions."*

~ DALAI LAMA XIV

Question 1:
What Am I Feeling?

Identifying your emotions is an important first step to managing your mood. By identifying your emotion, you can evaluate it and decide what to do with it. Too often, we over-generalize our emotional state as "bad" or "mad." In reality, feeling "bad" has many meanings. When you say, "I feel bad," you could mean "I feel sad," or "I feel lonely," or maybe, "I feel anxious," or even "I feel guilty." Similarly, "I am mad," could mean, "I am disappointed," or "I am irritated," or maybe "I am annoyed," or even "I am furious."

When you use a general word to express your emotions repeatedly, that term (and emotion) becomes stronger and feels heavier and heavier. This makes it more difficult to change your mood or let go of your unwanted feelings. When you identify the specific emotion, it becomes smaller, lighter, and much easier to let go.

Here's an example to help you understand this idea clearly. Imagine a moving day—the day you pack your household in preparation to move. Imagine putting everything from your bedroom (your bed, a dresser, a closet full of clothes, etc.) into one gigantic box and label it "bedroom." Would you be able to move the box easily? Would it be easy or difficult to find individual items within this box quickly? When you need to retrieve an item and look inside that box, does it look easy—or is it overwhelming or daunting?

Instead of one gigantic box, what if you separated your belongings into many little boxes and labeled them correctly? Imagine having 20-30 clearly labelled boxes: winter clothes, shoes, books, games, and so on. If you need to move one of those boxes, would you be able to move it easily? What if you need to find a pair of shoes? Wouldn't it be easy to grab the box labeled "shoes" and open it?

The same is true with your mood. When you pack your emotions under one big label, they remain cluttered, heavy, and unmanageable. Instead, take a second to identify your emotions and decide what you want to do with them.

It's easy for Beth and Amie to blame the other person to feel justified in their anger. However, when they looked inward, they discovered a range of emotions and options for handling them.

Beth reported feeling angry, disrespected, disappointed, resentful, violated, frustrated, unloved, misunderstood, taken advantage of, and unappreciated.

Amie reported feeling confused, angry, annoyed, disappointed, sad, afraid, helpless, unloved, accused, misunderstood, and frustrated.

Beth discovered her strongest emotions were feeling disrespected and taken advantage of, while Amie felt confused and frustrated.

REMEMBER: When you identify your specific emotion, it becomes smaller, lighter, and much easier to let go.

Did you know that there are over several hundred words in the English dictionary to describe emotions? Yet, most people use only eight to ten words to describe how they feel. The words I most often hear in my practice when I ask a client to describe how they feel about their problems are: bad, sad, angry, hurt, disappointed, anxious, and scared.

When you use one word to express an emotion repeatedly, that emotion feels big and difficult to change. To help you let go of a negative emotion easier, get specific with your words and challenge yourself to use a different label each time. Get creative, have fun, and get ready to be amazed to discover just how much control you do have over your emotions.

On the next few pages are a list of common emotions. This is not a complete list of all emotions, just a select few to get you to think about different ways to express yourself. On the list, I left out many words that might make you feel worse because they imply judgment or suggest that something is wrong with you. The idea is to keep your emotion as light as you can while expressing your feelings. This will help your mind release it faster.

Accused	Afraid	Aggravated
Aggressive	Agitated	Alienated
Alone	Ambivalent	Annoyed
Antsy	Anxious	Apprehensive
Attacked	Awkward	Baffled
Beat	Bitter	Blamed
Bleak	Blocked	Bored
Bothered	Bruised	Bummed
Burdened	Burned	Cheated
Combative	Concerned	Conflicted
Confused	Crabby	Cranky
Criticized	Cross	Crummy
Crushed	Deceived	Defeated
Defenseless	Deflated	Deprived
Despair	Detached	Disappointed
Disconnected	Discouraged	Disgruntled
Disillusioned	Dismay	Disorganized
Displeased	Disrespected	Dissatisfied
Distress	Disturbed	Doubtful
Down	Drained	Dread
Edgy	Embarrassed	Empty

Enraged	Excluded	Exhausted
Fear or fearful	Fidgety	Flustered
Forced	Fragile	Framed
Frantic	Frightened	Frustrated
Furious	Gloomy	Grouchy
Grumpy	Guarded	Guilty
Gullible	Heated	Heavy
Helpless	Hesitant	Hindered
Horrible	Horrified	Hostile
Humbled	Hurt	Icky
Ignored	Impatient	Inconvenienced
Indecisive	Indifference	Ineffective
Inhibited	Insecure	Insulted
Invalidated	Irked	Irrational
Irritated	Isolated	Jaded
Jealous	Judged	Jumpy
Lazy	Leery	Limited
Lonely	Loopy	Lost
Low	Mad	Manipulated
Meek	Miserable	Misled
Mistaken	Misunderstood	Moody
Neglected	Nervous	Numb
Offended	Overwhelmed	Perplexed
Pissed	Pooped	Pressured
Provoked	Puzzled	Rattled
Regretful	Resentful	Responsible
Restless	Ridiculed	Ridiculous
Robbed	Ruffled	Scared
Self-Conscious	Sensitive	Sheepish

Shocked	Shook up	Sick
Skeptical	Sorrow	Sorry
Spiteful	Startled	Strained
Stressed	Stuck	Stumped
Suppressed	Suspicious	Tense
Terrified	Threatened	Thrown
Trapped	Uncertain	Undermined
Unhappy	Unhinged	Unsure
Uptight	Vulnerable	Weigh down
Wired	Withdrawn	Worn

Let's have some fun with slang words from urbandictionary.com

Bent	Blown	Butt-hurt
Cheesed-off	Cut	Driddy
Durpy	Furt	Limp
Peeved	Petro	Poxy
Salty	Shut-down	Skerred
Stumb	Wacked	Wrecked

It's your turn to come up with other words you can use to describe your negative emotions. Think of words you use and words you have heard other people use and make your own list. You can even make up words if you like. I have a client, Helen, who used to say, "I'm so stupid," whenever she made a mistake, and that statement made her feel terrible about herself. After going through this exercise, Helen decided to make up her own words and now says, "Abba tea toe tea" and laughs it off whenever she makes a mistake. Those words she made up make no sense and are so funny, she and others can't help but shake it off and move on. In fact, a few of her friends are now using the same words to keep things light so they, too, can move on.

"Remember, happiness doesn't depend upon who you are or what you have, it depends solely upon what you think."

~ DALE CARNEGIE

CHAPTER THREE

Question 2:
Why Do I Feel This Way?

A nswering this question will give you insight into your mood and insight into yourself. As with the first question, this question allows you to sort your emotions and helps you to release the negative feelings that are holding you back so you can focus on reclaiming your happiness.

How many times have you said, "I don't know why I feel [insert your emotion here]? I just do." Or maybe you've said, "I am really anxious right now, but I don't know why."

When you say, "I don't know why," in response to someone's question about your feelings, it may be an automatic answer because you don't want to talk about it. Or, perhaps, you really don't understand your feelings because you haven't stopped to examine them.

When you respond in this manner, you are basically claiming, "I am powerless. My feelings are beyond my understanding and control." By not understanding why you feel the way you do, you become a victim of your feelings. You also place yourself in a situation of being powerless to change it.

You might wonder, "But I really don't know why I feel the way I do. Does that mean I am powerless?" Not at all. If you stop and look inward, you will find the reason for why you feel the way you do.

In life, there are only three causes for upset feelings, and they are very simple:

1. Unmet expectations
2. Thwarted intentions: something that stops or keeps you from what you've intended to do or have happened
3. A miscommunication or misunderstanding that leads to #1 or #2 above

Understanding the causes of your upset feelings will help you break free from your burden.

The next time you are having a relationship challenge, take a deep breath in and ask yourself:

1. What were my expectations in this situation and were they met?
2. Were my expectations realistic for this situation? Remember, just because you want things a certain way, doesn't mean it's realistic.
3. What were my intentions and did something happen that prevented me from completing my intentions?
4. Did I communicate my expectations or intentions to others clearly?

5. Did I understand the expectations or intentions of the other person(s)?

When you answer these questions honestly, you will find the reason for your upset feeling. Once you identify your emotion and the reason behind it, you reclaim your power to do something about it. From a place of understanding and strength, you can decide what to do that is best suited to create the results you want.

Beth feels entitled to her sense of being disrespected and taken advantage of. After all, Amie knew her curfew time but continued to disrespect it. Beth has tried to avoid a fight by speaking calmly to Amie, but rather than appreciating this, Amie took advantage of her kindness and continued to show a lack of care.

When Beth stops to reflect on the reasons for her upset feeling, she discovers:

1. *She expected Amie to follow the previously stated curfew time, and her expectation was not met.*
2. *She felt her expectation was realistic for this situation.*
3. *Her intention was to avoid a fight. Amie's continued disrespect made it hard for her to continue to be kind and understanding.*
4. *She realized she did not communicate her expectations clearly. She realized when she said, "I am not happy when you come home late. It would be nice if you came home at 10 p.m. I*

could trust and respect your decisions more that way," without enforcing previous consequences, she opened up the situation for interpretation and confusion.

5. *She wasn't aware of Amie's expectations or intentions.*

Amie feels confused and frustrated about what happened. She doesn't understand why her mom is enraged and accuses her of being selfish, untrustworthy, and causing her pain when she made a conscious decision to make her mom proud tonight. Amie thought they came to a new understanding about her curfew after the last fight when she begged her mom for some leeway. Since her mom started acting "cool" when Amie came home at 11 p.m., Amie assumed that was the new curfew time. Tonight, she decided to surprise her mom by coming home early.

When Amie examines her feelings, she discovered:

1. *She expected her mom to be happy that she came home twenty minutes earlier than she had been lately.*

2. *She came home a little earlier than 11 p.m. to show her mom she could be responsible for her decisions. She was proud of herself for making this decision and was expecting her mom to show appreciation and encouragement.*

3. *She did not communicate her intentions or expectations. She never confirmed the new curfew time. She was just happy that they were not fighting anymore and that her mother was*

beginning to see her as capable of making smart decisions for herself.

Amie realizes that she did not fully understand her mom's expectations. Even though her mom had said, "It would be nice if you came home by 10 p.m.," Amie decided that was only a guideline since there were no consequences like before.

"All that we are is the result of what we have thought. The mind is everything. What we think, we become."

~ BUDDHA

CHAPTER FOUR

Question 3:
Is This Emotion Useful for Any Reason?

So many emotions have no purpose other than to burden you and keep you stuck in a cycle of misery or pain. Other emotions have awesome purposes and can lead you down the path to your greatest and happiest self.

Have you ever known someone who is highly sensitive and cries easily when they are upset? What about someone who gets angry at the slightest thing? How about a person who is so anxious that it's difficult for them to do things that are simple for most people? Maybe you know someone like that, or maybe that someone is you, and you don't know what to do. Perhaps you've been stuck in this vicious cycle of heavy, negative feelings for so long you don't know how to get out of it. Maybe you have been told too many times that "you're just sensitive," or "you have an anger issue," or perhaps you've been told, "you have social anxiety," or that "you're a moody person."

Hearing labels like this repeatedly may have caused you to believe them. Because you believe them to be true, you might think this is who you are, and you can't change it.

You are NOT your feeling. Your feelings do not define who you are. You are NOT your feeling. Your feelings do not define who you are. In fact, you get to choose how you want to feel in every situation. If you have a feeling you do not want, you have the power to let that feeling go and choose a healthier, more empowering feeling instead. You can choose a healthier, more empowering feeling instead.

There are many times that you might have a negative emotion, but that emotion is useful as a learning tool. When you feel that your emotion is useful as a learning tool, you can embrace the moment and decide on a course of action that will bring you the results you want. Often, this too requires you to identify your emotions to focus on the lessons and your desired outcome.

In the case of Beth and Amie, they both decided that their emotions were weighing them down, causing increased tension in their relationship, and are not useful for any purpose. They both want to have a better relationship.

REMEMBER: *You are NOT your feelings. They do not define who you are.*

When you have a feeling you don't want, stop and evaluate it. Once you identify what you're feeling and why you feel that way, as well as if that feeling is useful for any reason, you will have a much more complete picture of what's going on. From there, you can take charge of your emotions to create the result you want.

*"For every minute you are angry,
you lose sixty seconds of happiness."*

~ AUTHOR UNKNOWN

CHAPTER FIVE

Question 4:
How Can I See This Differently?

Have you ever made a mistake that you regret and feel guilty about? The scenario might replay in your head repeatedly, and you feel terrible about it. The next thing you know, you are thinking about other mistakes you've made, and the regret and guilt become heavier and even overwhelming. It's like watching a train wreck happening right in front of you and feeling helpless to change the situation.

Have you also noticed that whatever you focus on grows bigger and bigger? Focusing on a problem is like feeding it and giving it the power to grow. If you don't want your problem to grow, you can choose to focus your energy and attention on something different. This can be easily accomplished when you ask yourself, "How can I see this differently?" When you ask yourself, "How can I see this differently?" you are actively challenging yourself to find different ways of looking at the same situation.

It is very easy to answer the question, "How can I see this differently?" with "I don't know," or "There is no other way to see this situation differently." I encourage you to use your imagination, be creative, and have fun coming up with different answers. The answers you come up with could be something very appropriate for the situation, or it could be something totally ridiculous that makes you laugh. The idea is to shift your mind away from the negative thoughts and feelings you currently have and into a more positive direction that allows you to take charge of your situation. Remember, whatever you focus your attention on becomes bigger. You have the power to shift your attention away from the problem and toward solutions instead.

Beth realizes that she was not clear in her communication with Amie. She further realizes that her sudden lack of discipline could send Amie the message that she was okay with the new curfew time.

Amie realizes that she has conveniently decided on the new curfew time without clarifying with her mother. Although she still feels her mother overreacted, Amie can see why her mother might feel disrespected and taken advantage of.

REMEMBER: *Whatever you focus on grows bigger and bigger. Focusing on a problem is like feeding it and giving it the power to grow. STOP feeding the things you no longer want and start focusing on what you want instead.*

"The greatest part of our happiness depends on our dispositions, not our circumstances."

~ MARTHA WASHINGTON

CHAPTER SIX

Question 5:
Would I Rather Be Right or Happy?

As simple as it may sound, the key to your happiness is simply choosing to be happy instead of fighting, defending, or pushing the other person to accept that you are right.

Choosing to be right gives you only one option. Because you are right, the other person or people are therefore wrong. It is very difficult to be happy with this option because it places the control and power outside of yourself. Since it is someone else's fault, and you can't change the other person, there is nothing you can do other than stew in your negative emotions while being "right."

When you choose to be right, it might seem as if you have won. Even if you "won" the argument, you are probably still not happy because when you force your opinions and thoughts onto someone, you do not restore balance and harmony to the relationship. The negative energy persists.

When you choose to be happy, you open yourself up to options and new possibilities. While you might not be one hundred percent happy with the outcome, you can be happy enough in that moment. That does not mean you have to settle. It just means that for right now, you choose to let go of the negative feeling and focus on a win-win outcome for all involved. When things settle, and emotions are in check, you can calmly bring the topic back up and express your thoughts and feelings in a clear way that helps you get your point across. When you express yourself calmly and clearly, the other person is more likely to hear you out. You are much more likely to get the outcome you are looking for.

Choosing happiness puts the power back into your hands. It allows you to take actions on your behalf, so you can maintain your peace and avoid negative feelings. Choosing happiness allows you to preserve and enhance your relationships while you continue to work toward the best outcome for yourself and those you love.

In the past, both Beth and Amie chose to be right and stood firm on their grounds because both parties saw compromising as "losing." They were both unhappy with the outcome of their continued fights and the increasing rift in their relationship. However, both mother and daughter felt powerless to change because the problem was the other person.

Using the 5 simple questions as a guide, Beth and Amie decided to let go of their unwanted negative emotions and worked toward understanding each other and rebuilding their relationship.

"Would I rather be right or happy?" is the most powerful question you can ask yourself when you're deciding on what to do with your negative emotion. This question serves as a reminder to choose happiness. In fact, this question is so powerful that you can use it alone most of the time and still get the result you're looking for. If you have difficulty choosing happiness by using this question alone, you can go back and start with questions one through four. By the time you arrive at the fifth question, your mind will be more open and accepting of happiness.

REMEMBER: *When you choose to be happy, you open yourself up to options and new possibilities.*

Section 2:
More Case Studies

"Most people are about as happy as they make up their minds to be."

-~ ABRAHAM LINCOLN

CHAPTER SEVEN

More Case Studies

L et's look at more scenarios of actual clients of mine and see how they've used the 5 simple questions to change their mood by letting go of their negative feelings to become happy. In these scenarios, I present only pertinent information as it relates to how these clients used the 5 simple questions. I left non-pertinent information out to avoid confusion and keep these examples brief and on point.

Scenario 1
Christina and her mother, Amanda.

Seventeen-year-old Christina staggered home drunk after being out all night. When her mother, Amanda, opened the door and saw the condition that Christina was in, she was speechless.

After the initial shock, Amanda started shouting at Christina. Realizing that Christina was too intoxicated for a conversation, Amanda sent her to her room to sleep it off.

Amanda planned on speaking to Christina in the morning after she sobered up.

Amanda already caught Christina smelling of alcohol a couple of times that semester. When Amanda asked her about it, Christina brushed it off and said she only tried a sip of beer. She reassured her mother that she was too smart to drink. Amanda felt comforted by the answer and did not push it further. After all, Christina was doing well in school and seemed generally happy.

When Christina came home drunk that night, Amanda was outraged. The outrage continued the next morning as mother and daughter sat down to discuss what had happened. Amanda did her best to stay calm during the conversation.

Christina made little eye contact during the conversation and insisted that she did not understand what the big deal was when "everyone else is doing it."

Christina exclaimed, "I am seventeen and a half, and in six months I will be an adult and can do whatever I want. Why can't you be realistic and just accept that I have the right to make my own decisions?"

Hearing this, Amanda's anger escalated, and she started yelling at Christina non-stop. A thirty-minute lecture ensued, ending with Amanda grounding Christina for a month. In addition, Amanda banned Christina from going out with her friends who were "doing it too." To show Christina how serious she was, Amanda took away her car key and cell phone.

Christina angrily stormed off, threw her lamp across her room, and blasted her music loudly. Amanda was left feeling scared and unsure of how to handle the situation.

Amanda was in a state of disbelief. She was consumed with worries. Questions such as, "What road has my daughter chosen to take? How can she be so irresponsible? What will her life be like if she continues down this path? Where did I go wrong?" flooded Amanda's mind. Images of everything bad that could happen to Christina while she was drunk flashed before Amanda's eyes. The possibilities of Christina hurting herself or someone else brought Amanda to tears.

In the following weeks, Christina tried to get her mother to ease the punishment by attempting to downplay the situation. This worried Amanda even more as she became convinced that Christina did not understand the effects of her actions and the horrific consequences they could have.

With each failed attempt, Christina became angrier and angrier at her mom. Their relationship was becoming worse by the day. Christina became withdrawn, both at home and at school. She refused to talk to her mom, do her chores, or complete her homework. Amanda sought help because she was concerned about Christina's behavior and was uncertain of how to resolve the situation.

Let's see how Christina and Amanda applied the 5 simple questions to reclaim their happiness and mend their relationship.

Question 1: What Am I Feeling?

When Amanda examines her feelings, she realizes that she feels:

1. Fearful: I'm so afraid that Christina is making a horrible mistake, and this mistake can ruin her life.
2. Overwhelmed: There's just so much negativity, anger, and resentment in the household that I don't know what to do.
3. Guilty: How could I not see the warning signs? I caught her with alcohol on her breath on two occasions and ignored the problem. She also started making new friends and was more withdrawn this year. Why didn't I see it? Why didn't I intervene?
4. Inept: I'm her mother. I'm responsible for raising her properly. Maybe I didn't do enough for her. She wouldn't be this way if I had paid more attention to her.
5. Powerless: She's so angry with me. We can't even have a conversation. How can I fix this if we can't even talk?

When Christina examines her feelings, she realizes that she feels:

1. Injustice: Mom has such double standards. She drinks with her friends all the time. In fact, just last weekend she came home tipsy.
2. Angry: Mom is so unfair. This is her problem, not mine. I only had a couple of beers. What's the big deal? Other kids my age were drinking so much

more. She should be happy I'm responsible enough to stop at two drinks.

3. Frustrated: Can't she see that I'm an adult? I can make my own decisions, and she has to accept that.

4. Defiant: I should just move out on my own. I'm almost eighteen anyway. I don't need this crap.

Question 2: Why Am I Feeling This Way?

Looking at each specific emotion above, Amanda identified several areas of unmet expectations and miscommunications. Amanda realized she expected that her daughter was smart enough to know that underage drinking is illegal and that it is not acceptable in her household. She also expected that, because of her parenting, Christina would adopt the same values and behaviors. Amanda realized that a large part of her fear about Christina's future stemmed from her own bad choices as a teenager.

Miscommunication also played a large part in their problem. Amanda disciplined Christina because she wanted her to understand the seriousness of the situation. Amanda's aim has always been to help her daughter grow up to be a healthy, responsible, and happy adult. Instead of creating a situation for learning and growing, the yelling, threats, and punishment had only caused a deterioration in their relationship, which further escalated the problems.

When Christina stopped and evaluated her emotions, she too found several areas of unmet expectations and miscommunications. First, Christina expected that her mother would not make such a big deal about her getting drunk because Amanda was actually a pretty cool mom who also liked to drink and party with her friends. Maybe a stern lecture, but not grounding her and taking away her social life for a month. Second, Christina felt that since she was almost eighteen, she should be allowed to make her own decisions. She conveniently ignored the fact that it is illegal for her to drink until she is twenty-one years old.

As for miscommunication, the moment she was grounded, Christina got angry and defended her case, rather than taking the time to understand where her mother was coming from. Instead of taking responsibility for her actions, Christina tried to exert her independence and anger by throwing things around and blatantly ignoring Amanda. Christina agreed that her behaviors added to the problem rather than resolving it.

Question 3: Is This Emotion Useful for Any Reason?

Even though both Christina and Amanda agreed that these emotions were useful as a starting point to discuss and resolve their differences, they both realized that there was no point in holding on to the fear, anger, or resentment. They are both willing to work on letting their negative emotions go and creating a happy solution for everyone.

Question 4: How Can I See This Differently?

While Amanda understood that Christina is going through a typical teenage period, where drinking alcohol is starting to be 'cool' for many, the seriousness of that decision still needed to be addressed. Instead of thinking and focusing on all the worst-case scenarios about Christina's life being destroyed, and going into fear and overwhelm, Amanda could have used her energy to come up with effective ways to communicate with her daughter in a way that creates trust while still standing firm to her rules. Amanda could also understand the double standard message she was portraying by coming home tipsy herself.

Amanda reminded Christina that there was a long family history of alcoholism and explained that her fear was largely based on that. In addition, Amanda revealed to Christina some trouble of her own teen years to help Christina understand where her fear came from.

Being reminded of the family history and hearing the stories of Amanda's troubled past helped Christina to understand her mother's reaction and allowed her to feel closer to her mother. Christina finally understood that her mother's fear and reactions came from a place of deep love and concern for her safety and happiness.

In addition, when she examined her own reactions, Christina could see how her actions amplified her mother's concerns and caused a further rift in their relationship.

Question 5: Would I Rather Be Right or Happy?

Having an honest and open conversation helped both mother and daughter release their anger and frustration. Both Amanda and Christina know that there is some work ahead to mend their relationship, but both felt positive and confident knowing that they can put their differences aside and rebuild their relationship.

The 5 simple questions is a powerful tool to help you understand your emotions and resolve arguments or disagreements in a more positive and productive way—a way that preserves, and even enhances relationships.

Scenario 2
Amanda vs. Amanda.

Now that you have seen how the 5 simple questions can be used to resolve arguments with others, let's see how you can use these same five questions to help you release negative feelings you might be holding against yourself.

Let's look at the example above again and see how Amanda used these 5 simple questions to release her self-judgments.

Amanda realized that besides the negative feelings she held against Christina, she held a significant amount of judgments against herself. These negative self-judgments were clouding her ability to parent, causing her to doubt her efforts, and second guess her actions. This led to poor sleep quality, less energy during the day to focus on her work, and general unhappiness.

To release her self-judgment and reclaim her happiness, Amanda applied the 5 simple questions to herself.

Question 1: What Am I Feeling?

1. Fearful: I'm so afraid that Christina is making a horrible mistake, and this mistake can ruin her life.
2. Overwhelmed: There's just so much negativity, anger, and resentment in the household that I don't know what to do.
3. Guilty: How could I not see the warning signs? I caught her with alcohol on her breath on two occasions and ignored the problem. She also started making new friends and was more withdrawn this year. Why didn't I see it? Why didn't I intervene?
4. Inept: I'm her mother. I'm responsible for raising her properly. Maybe I didn't do enough for her. She wouldn't be this way if I had paid more attention to her.
5. Powerless: She's so angry with me, we can't even have a conversation. How can I fix this if we can't even talk?

Question 2: Why Do I Feel This Way?

Amanda realized a lot of her negative self-judgments, fear, and guilt were based on the mistakes she had made as a teenager. Amanda didn't realize how much pressure and expectations she had placed on Christina because she didn't want her to make the same mistakes.

Question 3: Is This Emotion Useful for Anything?

Amanda readily saw how harmful it was to hold these judgments against herself. There is no purpose for hanging on to those emotions.

Question 4: How Can I See This Differently?

Amanda realized her self-judgments as being inept and powerless were not true and only served to increase her overwhelm and fear. Amanda has been doing a fantastic job as a mother, sacrificing so much so that Christina could have a great life. Amanda realized that regardless of how she parents, Christina is her own person and will make mistakes as she learns to understand who she is and creates her own value system. Amanda also realized she could improve her parenting and help Christina to make better decisions by explaining the reasons behind her rules, instead of saying "because that's what I expect."

Question 5: Would I Rather Be Right or Happy?

This one was easy for Amanda. She chose happiness for herself and her daughter.

Using the 5 simple questions, Amanda easily let go of her negative self-judgments, which allowed her to be happier and more productive, both at work and at home.

Scenario 3
Kelly vs. Kelly

Seventeen-year-old Kelly lost her virginity to an older man she had met at the library a month ago. At first, Kelly ignored Steve's attempts to talk to her. Steve's persistence paid off, and they began chatting when she took a break from her studies. Steve was nice and always made a point to compliment Kelly for both her intelligence and beauty. When Steve asked Kelly for a date, she declined. Steve was much older, and Kelly wasn't sure how sincere he was.

Day after day, Steve would show up at the library just to talk to Kelly. There was never any pressure, just nice friendly chats. After two weeks of this, Kelly decided it was okay to take a walk with him around the lake by the library.

Kelly was surprised by how much fun she had just talking with him. Steve showed genuine interest and care for Kelly. Toward the end of the walk, Steve pulled Kelly close for a kiss. Kelly really enjoyed the kiss and the budding romance between the two of them.

The following week, Steve confessed that he was thinking of her non-stop and has, in fact, fallen in love with her. Kelly was so happy because she knew she had fallen for Steve also. That week, Kelly skipped her library studies so she could go on dates with Steve.

Kelly knew that her parents would disapprove of Steve because of his age, so she kept him a secret from both her parents and her friends. That made the whole romance even more exciting. Steve and Kelly were sharing a secret that only the two of them knew of.

When Steve asked her to skip school the following Monday so they could spend the entire day together, Kelly was elated. She could not think about anything but spending time with Steve. He picked her up promptly at seven-thirty a.m. from her high-school parking lot and brought her to a fancy hotel. He said he wanted to pamper her and give her all the special things she deserved.

That morning, they ordered room service for breakfast, something Kelly has never done before. Steve was so classy and unlike any of the boys Kelly had dated. After breakfast, they went to the beach and picked seashells and played in the water.

After lunch, they went back to the hotel to snuggle up and watch a movie. The cuddling turned into intense kissing and ended up with Kelly agreeing to have sex with Steve. The day was so perfect in every way; Kelly never wanted it to end.

When Steve took Kelly back to school, he kissed her gently and said he couldn't wait to see her at the library again tomorrow. Steve also asked Kelly to think about how she would like to spend their next date together.

Kelly was on cloud nine for the rest of the day. She replayed the beautiful details of their romantic day and lovemaking over and over in her mind.

The next day, Kelly couldn't concentrate on her classes. She continued to fantasize about their next date and couldn't wait to tell Steve about what she wanted to do.

Kelly excitedly ran up the library steps right after school. She knew Steve would be right at the entrance waiting for her just like he had for the past three weeks. When she got to the entrance, Steve wasn't there. Kelly waited and waited. After two hours and endless texts, Steve was still nowhere to be found. Kelly was beside herself with worry but knew she had to go home.

This scene repeated itself for the rest of the week. Kelly would anxiously text Steve every chance she had. To her dismay, there was no answer. Kelly realized that she got so swept up in the secrecy of their romance that she didn't know any of his friends nor where he lived. Kelly felt so helpless. She didn't know what to do or who she could talk to. She was certain that something bad had happened to her love. She contemplated talking to her mother and asking for her help, but the fear of getting in trouble stopped her.

That Friday, as Kelly was sitting at her usual spot in the library waiting for Steve, she overheard a girl talking to her friend about an older man she had met earlier last week. Between tears, the girl told her friend about how this older man had tricked her into sex by sweeping her off her feet. Her description of the man and his actions matched Steve to a tee. Even the term of affection that Steve had called her, "doll face" was the same.

Kelly's heart sank, and she knew she too had been duped by this man. She ran out of the library in tears. Kelly was in a state of shock. She realized she had been used. She had foolishly trusted a man she barely knew. Kelly was angry at herself for being so stupid and naïve. She did not know what to do or whom to turn to. Talking to her parents was out of the question—she dreaded the consequences of her parents finding out she had lost her virginity. She dreaded the consequences of her actions even more. Lost in the special romantic moment, Kelly had agreed to unprotected sex. The possibilities of pregnancy and sexually transmitted diseases frightened her.

For the next few weeks, all Kelly could do was cry and sleep. Kelly's parents tried to talk to her, but she would not tell them anything. Luckily, Kelly agreed to talk to a professional, and her parents brought her in for help.

Kelly was reluctant to share much at first. After much reassurance, Kelly opened up and shared what had happened. She recalled that her shock quickly turned into sadness, which quickly turned into anger. She was angry at him for tricking her and angry at herself for being stupid.

Kelly didn't think she would be willing or able to let go of her anger. In fact, she was scared to let go of her anger because she was afraid that she would be duped again if she let her guard down. After some reassurance, Kelly was willing to use the 5 simple questions to help her be happy again.

Question 1: What Am I Feeling?

When Kelly examined her feelings, she reports feeling angry (at herself and Steve), disappointed, and fearful of the consequences.

Question 2: Why Am I Feeling This Way?

Kelly identified all three causes of upset as the reasons for her feeling of anger, disappointment, and fear. The first and biggest reason was unmet expectations. She had fully trusted Steve and expected that he was honest and true to his words. She had expected that they were a couple who deeply cared about each other and that the lovemaking was a natural aspect of sharing that love.

As for miscommunication, Steve had purposefully led Kelly on and manipulated her. However, Kelly acknowledged that she made a lot of assumptions based on his actions. Not once did they have a talk about being exclusive or real future plans. Kelly realized she had romanticized a lot and created a romance that was, in fact, amplified by her constant daydreaming.

Thwarted intentions also came into play for Kelly. Kelly had fully intended on carrying on this forbidden romance and had come up with several scenarios of how they could make this relationship work. His lies and deceit thwarted her intentions of a happily-ever-after.

Question 3: Is This Emotion Useful for Any Reason?

At first, Kelly truly believed that holding on to the anger, disappointment, and fear would help her learn her lesson and prevent her from making the same mistake in the future. After examining the situation further, Kelly realized she was only torturing herself by hanging on to these emotions. She realized she had already learned her lesson and felt certain she would not repeat the same mistake. These negative emotions then only served to hold her back and rob her of her confidence and joy.

Question 4: How Can I See This Differently?

Kelly had to come to terms with the situation. Instead of continuing to beat herself up, Kelly decided to accept that she made a mistake for trusting someone she hardly knew. However, that mistake did not make her naïve or stupid. The fact was, this older man preyed on young girls. He was so kind and attentive that it was hard to know he was insincere. Kelly agreed that blaming herself and holding onto the anger and disappointment would only prevent her from healing and moving forward.

Additionally, Kelly could see the potential danger of keeping this to herself. Although Kelly knew it would upset her parents, she also knew just how much they loved her. Kelly needed her parents' support and guidance now more than ever. After all, she had unprotected sex with a stranger who was likely having unprotected sex with other girls. Kelly needed to take care of her physical health as well as her emotional health. At the end of the session, Kelly agreed to share the whole story with her parents.

Rather than continuing to see her parents as a source of potential problems, Kelly decided to see her parents as true allies.

Question 5: Would I Rather Be Right or Happy?

Kelly decided that there was no point in beating herself up any longer. Yes, she had fallen for his tricks, but the man was a master manipulator. Kelly decided that it was time to let go of the anger and disappointment toward herself and embraced the situation as a powerful learning lesson.

Kelly decided to forgive herself and focus her energy and attention back on things that bring her joy.

After talking with her parents, Kelly felt even closer to them than before. One great thing about this horrible situation is that it helped Kelly to remember just how much her parents love and support her.

Once Kelly decided to release her negative emotions and focus on her happiness, Kelly and her parents sought medical care and notified the police about Steve and his predatory actions. Kelly was reluctant to talk to the police at first because she did not much information on Steve and was afraid they wouldn't believe her. However, the officers she spoke with were very understanding and reassured her they would do everything they could to locate and charge Steve. Taking these steps put the power back into Kelly's hands and helped her let go of her fear and move forward.

"When you hold resentment toward another, you are bound to that person or condition by an emotional link that is stronger than steel.

Forgiveness is the only way to dissolve that link and get free."

~ CATHERINE PONDER

Section 3:
Get Ready to Reclaim
Your Happiness!

CHAPTER EIGHT

Get Ready to Reclaim Your Happiness

A re you ready to use the 5 simple questions to reclaim your happiness? You can use the next few pages to work through some challenges you're dealing with, so you can resolve them in a positive way.

Think of a recent fight or disagreement you had that you still hold a significant amount of negative feelings about. Remember, this is for you so answer the following questions honestly for yourself. To maximize your results, be creative as you answer the questions. Challenge yourself by putting yourself in the other person's shoes and see things from their perspective.

You can use the worksheets in the next few chapters to help you manage your moods. If you want to go even further, check out the *Companion Journal* to this book. This journal was designed to help

you understand, track, and take control of
your moods.

Write down all the important details of the disagreement.

_____

_____

_____

_____

_____

_____

_____

_____

_____

_____

_____

_____

_____

_____

_____

_____

_____

_____

_____

_____

_____

Question 1: What Am I Feeling?

For this exercise, it is important for you to focus on your feelings rather than your thoughts. The word "think" and "feel" are often used interchangeably, yet, there is an important distinction between them. A thought is defined by the Merriam-Webster dictionary as, "an idea or opinion produced by thinking or occurring suddenly in the mind." Whereas, a feeling is defined as, "an emotional state or reaction." Therefore, a thought refers to a mental process, and a feeling refers to an emotional process.

We frequently use vague terms to describe our feelings, and we commonly mistake thoughts for feelings; our true feelings are often not recognized. Thus, feelings tend to hide below the surface, tucked away so deeply in the subconscious part of your mind that even you are not aware of them. If you don't resolve your feelings, they will continue to hide in the background and affect how you think and act.

Here's an example to demonstrate why differentiating a feeling from a thought is important. Let's say you have a strong feeling of fear when it comes to snakes. Normally, when you think of snakes, you think, "snakes are so disgusting. It makes me sick to my stomach to even think about them." Today, you want to change that, so you changed your thoughts to, "Snakes are okay. I can think about them. It's no big deal." Well, that's a great attitude, but the moment you think about the snakes slithering near you, or thrusting their tongue out at you, you recoil in fear, your stomach turns, and you think, "This is not working. Snakes are disgusting."

If you changed your feeling from fear to neutral, your reactions would be different. When you feel neutral about snakes, you might have unpleasant thoughts about snakes here and there, but you can readily shake it off.

Since "feel" and "think" are often used interchangeably, how can you identify which you are dealing with?

Remember, feelings are emotional states. Examples of feelings you might experience are angry, sad, disappointed, scared, frustrated, stressed, lonely, rejected, or anxious.

Here are examples of thoughts you might have that sound like feelings:

- I feel she lied to me.
- I feel she was wrong.
- I feel that nothing would change, so why bother?
- I feel like I don't know how to fix this.

None of the previous four examples above reflect an emotional state. These are all mental processes.

One way to check to see if you're dealing with a feeling is to replace the word "feel" with the word "think." If the new sentence with the word "think" makes sense, chances are, you're dealing with a thought. If the new sentence makes little sense, it's likely that you're dealing with a feeling.

Let's look at a few examples.

"I feel I'm a disappointment to others," becomes, "I think I'm a disappointment to others." The new sentence makes sense, so it's likely a thought.

Here's another example of a thought that sounds like a feeling. "I feel that no one likes me." When you replace "feel" with "think" the new sentence becomes, "I think that no one likes me." Again, this sentence makes sense, so you're dealing with another thought.

Let's look at a true feeling statement, "I feel sad." When you replace "feel" with "think" you get, "I think sad." The new sentence doesn't make much sense, so the original sentence does, in fact, express a feeling.

When you realize you are dealing with a thought, how do you go further to discover the feeling behind it? To find your feeling, ask yourself, "and that makes me feel ___?" after each sentence you identified as a thought.

In the example above, "I think that no one likes me," you can add, "and that makes me feel ___." Let's say your answer is, "and that makes me feel lonely." Let's check this sentence to see if it is a feeling or thought.

When you replace "feel" with "think" you get, "I think lonely." This new sentence makes little sense. Therefore, you are dealing with a feeling.

Let's say your answer was "and that makes me feel that I can't trust anyone." Replacing "feel" with "think" you get, "and that makes me think I can't trust anyone." The new sentence makes sense, so you're dealing with another thought.

Keep asking yourself, "and that makes me feel___?" and analyzing it until you identify your feeling.

Another easy way to make sure you are dealing with a feeling is to complete the sentence, "I feel" with just one emotional word. You can go back to pages twelve to fourteen and pick a word or several words from the list that best describe your current emotional state.

Write down all the emotions you are feeling. Remember to be as specific as you can. Rather than staying with the generic, "I feel bad." Work on identifying your true feelings such as, "I feel hurt. I feel annoyed. I feel discouraged." You can also turn to pages twelve to fourteen and identify your specific emotions.

_____

_____

_____

_____

_____

_____

_____

_____

_____

_____

_____

_____

_____

_____

_____

_____

_____

_____

_____

_____

_____

Next, replace "feel" with "think" to see if you are truly
Next, replace "feel" with "think" to see if you are truly
dealing with a feeling. (You can skip this if you identified
your emotions from the list on pages twelve to fourteen.)

_____

_____

_____

_____

_____

_____

_____

_____

_____

_____

_____

_____

_____

_____

_____

_____

_____

_____

_____

_____

_____

_____

_____

_____

Question 2: Why Do I Feel This Way?

When you use this question with the intention of reclaiming your happiness, focus on identifying which of the three causes of upset you're dealing with, instead of justifying your emotions. Remember, all three of the causes might be involved. Here's a quick reminder of the three causes of upset feelings:

1. Unmet expectations
2. Thwarted intentions: something that stops or keeps you from what you've intended to do or to make happen
3. A miscommunication or misunderstanding that leads to #1 or #2 above

If you need a more detailed reminder of what the three causes of upset feelings are and why it's important to identify them, you can go back and review chapter three.

Here's an example of justifying your feelings. "I'm angry because she didn't return my sweater even though I asked for it three times."

Instead, you can say, "I'm angry because when I loaned her the sweater, I asked her to agree to return it to me on Friday. She did not meet the expectation that we had set."

Use the fill in the blanks below to list all your feelings and the reasons for your feelings.

I feel _____ because

_____

_____

_____

_____

_____

_____

_____

I feel _____ because

_____

_____

_____

_____

_____

_____

_____

I feel _____ because

_____

_____

_____

_____

_____

_____

_____

_____

Question 3: Is This Emotion Useful for Anything?

Initially, many people will say, "Yes, my negative emotion is useful," and they will say something similar to:

- I need to make the other person pay.
- I don't want to look weak.
- If I forgive them, they will do it again or think I'm stupid.
- I don't want to make the same mistake again.
- They hurt me so badly, and I can't just let it go.

In reality, holding onto negative emotions only hurts you. Think about it. When you hold onto your negative emotions, it feels heavy and burdensome. It makes it hard for you to think about something else or enjoy yourself. Do you really want to give someone else the power to control your happiness?

Forgiveness doesn't mean that you agree with what they did. Forgiveness means taking your power back and saying, "I am strong enough to let this go so I can be free to focus on what's important to me."

Ask yourself, is this emotion useful for any reason? If you answer yes, write down how it helps you. Then go back and review what you wrote and see if that is really the case. Does holding onto those negative feelings really free you and allow you to do the things you truly want to do?

_____

_____

_____

_____

_____

Question 4: How Can I See This Differently?

You already know how you feel about the situation so use your imagination to come up with creative ways to see the situation differently. Here are several ways to help you change your perspective quickly and easily.

1. For a moment, put yourself into the other person's shoes and see things from their perspective. Ask yourself, "What could be going on in this person's life that is causing them to think, feel, or react this way?"

2. If that's too hard to do, pick a person or even a made-up character that you admire, and imagine how they would see the situation. For example, "How would my dad think or feel about this situation?" or "How would Superman think or feel about this situation?"

3. You can also pretend you're watching a movie and the situation was a scene from that movie. How would you see that situation differently then?

4. Perhaps you can pretend that your very best friend or the person you love most just experienced your exact scenario. How would they view the situation? What would they do differently?

Use your imagination to create three different versions of how you can see this situation differently.

Version 1:

_____

_____

_____

_____

_____

_____

_____

_____

_____

_____

_____

_____

_____

_____

_____

_____

_____

_____

_____

_____

_____

Version 2:

Version 3:

Question 5: Would I Rather Be Right or Happy?

This question is hard for many people when they first read it because they think they are happy when they are right. There are many occasions where you are right and happy. However, when you're dealing with a negative emotion such as anger or disappointment, choosing to be right and holding onto your emotion also means that you give up your real happiness.

Think about it. When you choose to be right and hold on to your negative emotions, are you truly happy? Did you and the other person make-up and you both feel good about the outcome or do you still feel a sense of tension or disconnection between you and the other person?

Remember, being happy doesn't mean you have it your way. It means that you choose to put the differences aside or to let go of your negative emotions so you can focus on creating what you truly want instead.

Ask yourself, am I ready to give up feeling _____ so I can be happy instead?

If you answered, yes, the next chapter could help you reclaim your happiness.

If you answered no, ask yourself, what am I afraid would happen if I stopped feeling _____. Then go back and answer questions one to five again.

You deserve to be happy, and happiness is simply a choice! Whenever possible, choose happiness for yourself!

You might be wondering, "Okay, I have decided to be happy, but I don't feel any better. Now what? How can I actually let things go and move forward?"

Deciding to be happy is a crucial step to being happy. Once you've decided to be happy, then you can begin to take action to be happy. In section four, we will discuss three techniques you can use to reclaim your happiness.

When you forgive,
you in no way change the past –
but you sure do change the future."

~ BERNARD MELTZER

CHAPTER NINE

How to Be Happy

Whateway if you did, in fact, choose to be happy, but
you are still having a hard time letting go? What
can you do?

One way to be happy is to focus your attention and
energy on doing something you really enjoy. This tells your
mind that even though things aren't going the way you
want them to go, you are still the one in control of your
feelings and you can choose to do what makes you happy.

This is not the same as pretending that you are not
bothered and mope. This is actively choosing to do what
you love and feeding that positive energy to help it grow.

*REMEMBER: What you focus on grows
bigger and bigger. Rather than focusing
on the problem, focus on something you
enjoy and let that good feeling grow.*

Reclaim Your Happiness Option 1:

Write down as many things as you can think of that you enjoy doing that are fun or relaxing to you. Think of things that you can do that make you smile, laugh, or fill you with motivation, happiness, or positivity.

Here are some examples:

I enjoy watching funny cat videos, listening to music, reading a book, working out, going to the beach, talking to my friends, playing video games, dancing, and hiking.

Your Turn: Make a list of things you enjoy doing. Come up with as many as you can think of. When you want to reclaim your happiness, take a look at this list, pick out one or two things and do the things you enjoy.

Keep adding to this list as you find more things that bring you happiness.

_____

_____

_____

_____

_____

_____

_____

_____

_____

_____

_____

_____

Reclaim Your Happiness Option 2:

Another option is to be fully present with your problem. Start by recognizing and accepting that things aren't the way you want it to be. However, instead of sulking and allowing your emotions to control you, take charge. Ask yourself, "What would I like to see happen and what are one or two things I can do right now to move in that direction?" This puts the power back in your hands as you focus your energy on working toward a solution instead of feeling helpless or like a victim.

When you don't like your current situation, and you want to be happy, you can choose to focus on the solutions instead of the problem.

The first step is to decide how you would like to see this situation resolved. It would be nice if the situation got fixed or changed to your exact liking, but chances are, that might not happen right away. So instead, focus on your short-term goals.

Ask yourself, "What can I be happy enough with right now, knowing that this is only a beginning step toward my ultimate goal?"

Next, ask yourself, "What are one or two things I can do right now to move toward my desired outcome?"

_____

_____

_____

_____

_____

_____

_____

_____

_____

_____

_____

_____

_____

_____

_____

_____

_____

_____

_____

_____

_____

_____

Reclaim Your Happiness Option 3:

Another way you can create happiness and focus on the solutions is to use the "Start, Stop, and Continue" method.

First, you want to identify your short-term goals. Ask yourself, "What can I choose to be happy enough with right now, knowing that this is only a beginning step toward my ultimate goal?"

Second, ask yourself, "What could I choose to START doing to help me achieve my goals?"

Third, ask yourself, "What could I choose to STOP doing that would help me to achieve my goals?"

Fourth, ask yourself, "What could I choose to CONTINUE doing to help me achieve my goals?"

For example, let's say you and your mom have been fighting because she feels that you are not taking your schoolwork seriously. Let's also say that you are taking your schoolwork seriously, but you are struggling with math and you don't want to admit it, or don't know how to ask for help. Your mom is frustrated that your grade is slipping. You're trying your best, but you just don't get math and your mom's constant nagging weighs heavily on you, making it even harder to focus on your schoolwork.

Using the Start, Stop, and Continue method, you might create a plan that looks something like this: (Just jot down ideas or phrases. They don't have to be complete sentences.)

1. Short-term goal: bring my grade up from a C to a B in one month

2. START:
   - Ask the teacher for extra help and extra credit assignments
   - Talk to Mom about getting a tutor
   - Partner with other students to work together
3. STOP:
   - Stop procrastinating
   - Stop spacing out when things make little sense during the lecture
   - Stop pretending that I don't care about my grades
4. CONTINUE:
   - To do my best
   - To complete all assignments on time
   - To stay committed to my education

Use the next few pages to identify your goals and your START, STOP, and CONTINUE plan.

Step 1: What are my short-term goals?

_____

_____

_____

_____

_____

_____

_____

_____

_____

Step 2: What could I choose to START doing?

Step 3: What could I choose to STOP doing?

_____

_____

_____

_____

_____

_____

_____

_____

_____

_____

_____

_____

_____

_____

_____

_____

_____

_____

_____

_____

_____

_____

_____

_____

_____

Step 4: What could I choose to CONTINUE doing?

_____

_____

_____

_____

_____

_____

_____

_____

_____

_____

_____

_____

_____

_____

_____

_____

_____

_____

_____

_____

_____

_____

_____

_____

_____

_____

_____

Once you've created your happiness plan, regardless of which option you choose, the next step is to follow through. Take small, consistent steps daily, and you will start creating a healthier, happier outlook and positive habits for yourself. Like anything else, with practice, you'll find that it gets much easier to focus on positive solutions rather than hanging on to the bad feelings.

You now have some very simple yet effective tools that put the control and power back in your hands. What you do with this is up to you. I hope you recognize just how much power you have over your moods. Things that used to bother you in the past don't have to bother you anymore because you can let them go. Remember, you deserve to be happy and you can make it happen for yourself!

"It is possible to live happily in the here and the now. So many conditions of happiness are available – more than enough for you to be happy right now."

~ THICH NHAT HA

Companion Journal

This journal was created as a companion to the book, *5 Simple Steps to Manage Your Mood*. It was designed to help you develop a deeper understanding of your moods so you can take charge of your feelings with ease.

The first section will help you understand your moods by showing your current go-to feelings and reactions.

The second section will help you to track, analyze, and take charge of your mood for 21 days. Why 21 days? Research shows it takes 21 days of repetition to develop a new habit - your new go-to feelings and reactions. By completing this section, you will develop a powerful skill to be aware of your emotions and take positive actions for yourself.

The third section will help you use the five simple steps presented in the book to let go of any unwanted emotions.

You deserve to be happy with yourself and to enjoy happy, healthy relationships with others. Let's make it happen!

Sample Journal Prompts

Section One: Understanding Your Mood

- These are the words I often use to describe my feelings.
- Of these feelings, I have the hardest time letting go of .... because...
- These types of situations often push me into that mood:

Section Two: Tracking Your Mood

- Today, I choose to focus on feeling:
- My top 5 actions to achieve my desired feeling are:
- If I get upset, I will remind myself to let it go with the following words, phrases or actions:

Section Three: Taking Charge of Your Mood

- What were my expectations?
- What could I have done differently to understand their expectations or intentions?
- How might it turn out differently if I understood their expectations or intentions?

Sample Journal Pages

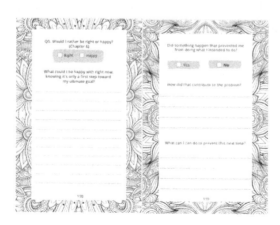

I would, but MY DAMN MIND won't let me

How many times have you been told by well-meaning parents, adults, or even your friends that you should just stop thinking or feeling a certain way? They tell you that the problems you have are all in your head. They tell you to stop making a big deal out of things, that you're too sensitive and there is no reason to be nervous or anxious. And yet you are. You don't know what to think or how to feel. You feel so tense and nervous. Others seem to have it so easy. But for you, life is difficult and so unfair!

Your situation may seem hopeless, and perhaps you have even concluded that you were just "born that way," and there is nothing you can do to change.

But what if you are wrong about that conclusion? What if there was a way for you to create the changes you desperately desire? What if I can teach you how to take control of your mind and be in charge of your thoughts and feelings? Would you want to learn how to do that for yourself?

The power of the human mind is incredible. It can create horrible life experiences, and it can create happy, successful ones too. It might not feel that way right now, but you do get to choose which life experiences you'll have. Once you learn easy, yet highly effective ways to take charge of your mind, you'll find that you have the power to create the life you want and deserve. The power to create permanent positive change is available to you no matter what you are struggling with currently. Stop wasting your energy and time on those old, useless emotions and thoughts. Today is the day to change your life experiences. This book will show you how to:

- Challenge your old negative belief patterns.
- Stop unhealthy thoughts and feelings.
- Create positive life experiences for yourself.
- Stay calm and in control in any situation.
- Unleash the power of your mind to create the life you want and deserve!

Everyone's journey to happiness begins with the belief that happiness is possible. Even if your personal experiences have led you to believe you are destined to have a difficult life filled with stress, anxiety, and unhappiness—I will show you that you have other options. You can learn to believe that happiness is possible for you. In this book, I will show you how to take charge of your mind to overcome your obstacles and struggles. I will show you simple yet powerful principles to strengthen your self-belief that leads to a solid foundation for happiness and success: so that the next time somebody asks you, "Why can't you just control yourself?" you can smile and thank them for the gentle reminder and instantly take control of your thoughts and feelings again. You are the key to your own success and happiness.

Now close your eyes and imagine for a moment how wonderful your life will be once you fully understand how to control your thoughts, feelings, and actions. If you are ready to make that dream life your reality, I encourage you to read this book with an open mind and a willingness to try something new. Get ready to be amazed at how quickly you can take charge of your life now!

Available in paperback, eBook and audiobook

Jump-Start Your Confidence and Boost Your Self-Esteem

D o you often feel as though other people are better than you? Does it seem they are more carefree, more outgoing, and more confident? They make friends easily and good things seem to happen for them all the time. They are fun, witty, and full of charm. Everywhere they go, people are drawn to them. They do what they want and say what they think.

These positive, likable traits seem to come so naturally for them. But for you, life is filled with anxiety, fear, and self-doubt. What is their secret? How can they talk to anyone about anything with ease, while it's a significant struggle for you to just be in the presence of others, let alone carry on a conversation?

You dream of being different. You dream of being comfortable in your own skin. You dream of creating meaningful relationships, going after what you want with confidence, and feeling happy and satisfied with your everyday life. But your fear, self-doubt may be holding you back, causing you to feel trapped and powerless to change your situation. You're left feeling sad, lonely, and insecure about yourself and your life.

What if there was a way to change all of that? What if you could destroy your fear and self-doubt and be strong and self-assured instead? What would it be like if you could go into any situation with excitement, courage, and confidence? Imagine what your life would look like and what you could achieve. Just imagine.

I'm will let you in on a little secret. That excitement, courage, and confidence which you admire in others are skills you can learn.

Sure, there are some people for whom these traits come naturally, but if you were not born with these traits, you can learn them. The thing is, you can learn to change your negative thinking, destroy your fear and self-doubt, and go after whatever you want with confidence. You can learn to be comfortable in your own skin and be completely at ease while expressing yourself.

You were born with incredible powers within yourself – powers I like to refer to as, Inner Superpowers (ISPs). When tapped into, these ISPs will help you be happy, resilient, and successful in life. The problem is that you have not been aware of these ISPs, nor how to use them.

Maybe you saw a glimpse of them here and there, but you didn't recognize their power or have faith in them. If you don't know what your Inner Superpowers are, how can you tap into them consistently and achieve the results you want and deserve?

In this book, you will learn:

- The seven Inner Superpowers guaranteed to destroy your fear and self-doubt.
- Create a strong sense of self-esteem and unshakable confidence.
- Easy to use tools to change your negative thinking into empowering thoughts.
- How to connect to and strengthen your Inner Superpowers.
- How to consistently tap into and unleash your Inner Superpowers whenever you want to.
- How to live within your full power and be happy, confident, and successful in life—and more!

You have so many Inner Superpowers that make you wonderful in every way. In this book, I have chosen to share seven specific ISPs because these seven are your best bet for destroying fear and self-doubt.

There is much written about each of these ISPs and each ISPs can be a stand-alone book. However, I know your time is valuable and you have other responsibilities and activities to tend to. This is why you'll find that these chapters are brief and to the point.

By reading this book and completing the activities within each section, you will learn how to consistently tap into these ISPs, to harness them, and unleash them whenever you want. You can learn how to confidently go after what you want and create that happy and successful life you've been dreaming about.

Available in paperback, eBook and audiobook

About the Author

Dear Reader,

If you are a teenager struggling with high stress, anxiety, self-doubt, low-confidence or depressive symptoms, I want you to know that you are not alone. I know because I have been there myself. My name is Jacqui Letran, and I have over eighteen years of experience helping thousands of teens, and I know I can help you!

I know you're frustrated, scared, and lonely. I was too. I also know confidence, success, and happiness are achievable because I have successfully freed myself from those old emotions and embraced my life with excitement, confidence, and joy. My goal is to help you understand the power of your mind and show you how you can master it to overcome your struggles and step into the magnificence of your own being, just like I did—and just like thousands of others have done using these same techniques.

Who I am and why I care.

My life was rather easy and carefree until I hit my teenage years. Overnight, it seemed that all my friends transformed from girls into women! They began to wear makeup and dressed in expensive and sexy clothes. They flirted with boys. Some even flaunted the older boys they were dating in front me. I, on the other hand, remained trapped in my boyish body. And, within the rules of my super-strict mother, wearing makeup, sexy clothes, or going on dates were not options for me.

I felt different and isolated—and I quickly lost all my friends. I didn't know what to say or how to act around others. I felt awkward and left behind. I just didn't fit in anymore. I became more and more withdrawn as I wondered what was wrong with me. Why didn't I blossom into a woman like all my friends? Why was life so difficult and so unfair?

- **I blamed my mother for my problems.** "If she weren't so strict, I would be allowed to date and have nice, sexy clothes," I thought. At least then I would fit in, and everything would be perfect!

- **I also felt very angry.** My life had taken a turn for the worst—but no one seemed to care or even notice. I started skipping school, began smoking, and getting into fights. I walked around with a chip on my shoulder and an "I don't care" attitude.

- **I felt invisible, unimportant, and unworthy.** Deep down, I only wanted to be accepted as I was. I wanted to belong. I wanted to be loved.

I thought my wishes were answered when I was sixteen. I meet a man five years older than me. He showered his love and affection on me and made me feel as if I was the most important person on earth. Six months later, I was a high school dropout, pregnant teen living on public assistance. I felt more alienated than ever before. Everywhere I went, I felt judged and looked down upon. I felt despair and was certain my life was over. I had no future. I knew I was destined to live a miserable life.

I felt truly alone in the world.

Except I wasn't alone; I had a baby growing inside me. The day I gave birth to my son and saw his angelic face, I knew that it was up to me to break this cycle of self-destructive thoughts and actions.

That's when everything changed!

I began to read every self-help book I could get my hands on. I was on a mission of self-discovery and self-love. I began to let go of the old beliefs that prevented me from seeing myself as capable, intelligent, and beautiful.

The more I let go of those old beliefs, the more confident I became, the more I accomplished. It was a powerful lesson in how changing my thoughts resulted in changing my life.

Six years later, at twenty-three, I earned my master's degree in nursing and became a Nurse Practitioner. Since then, I have dedicated over eighteen years of my life working in adolescent health. I love using my gift and passion to empower teens to create a bright future for themselves.

As I reflect on my painful teen years, I realize how I played a major role in determining my life experiences. My low confidence had paralyzed me from taking action, thus reinforcing my misguided belief that I was different or inferior.

I knew I had to share this knowledge to help teens avoid some of the pain I had experienced.

In my twenty-plus year career specializing in Adolescent Health, I have:

- Established, owned and operated Teen Confidence Academy, specializing in helping teens overcome stress, anxiety, and depressive symptoms without medication or long-term traditional therapy,
- Established, owned and operated multiple "Teen Choice Medical Center" locations,
- Become a Speaker, Podcaster and Multi-Award-Winning Author,
- Educated and supported thousands of teens and adults to overcome stress, anxiety and depressive symptoms,
- Raised a loving, intelligent, and confident man (he is my pride and joy), and
- Completed post-graduate training in holistic and alternative health and healing methods.

I am deeply passionate about helping teens let go of their barriers to see the beauty and greatness within themselves. I believe each of us deserves a life full of health, love, and happiness. I also believe that every person has within them all the resources needed to achieve a beautiful and fulfilling life.

When I was going through my troubled teen years, I needed a place where I could be mentored, where I could learn, reflect, and grow; a place where I could heal and get a proper, healthy perspective of myself and the world around me. I didn't have that option then, or at least I didn't know where to find it.

That is why I became a Mindset Mentor specializing in teen confidence, and that's why I am writing this book for you now.

Thousands of teens are living in quiet desperation right now because no one has shown them the key to their success. My goal in writing this book is to teach you about your mind so you can control your thoughts, feelings, and actions. You can take charge of creating the life that you want and deserve. You deserve to be successful and happy in life. Let's make it happen!

Jacqui Letran

Acknowledgements

I would like to express a heartfelt thank you to my best friend and husband, Joseph Wolfgram. Without his love, endless hours of revisions, and support, this book would not have been possible. Thank you for patiently listening to me talk about this book endlessly.

To my son, Alan Letran, thank you for being my biggest life teacher and a source of endless love.

To my family, thank you for believing in me and cheering me on. It means so much to me to have your love and support.

To my editor, Coral Coons, thank you so much for your professionalism and expert advice. You are a joy to work with.

To all of my clients, teachers, and mentors, whether in a professional relationship or in life experiences, a big thank you for being a part of my life. Your presence in my life has helped me grow and transform from a scared little girl into a confident, healthy, and happy woman.

Connect with Me

I love hearing from my readers.
Please feel free to connect with me at:

Amazon.com/Author/JacquiLetran
www.JacquiLetran.com
Facebook.com/JacquiLetran
Linkedin.com/in/JacquiLetran
Instagram.com/JacquiLetran

You can also contact me at:
Author@JacquiLetran.com

Thank you so much for reading.
If you enjoyed this book, please consider leaving an honest
review with your favorite online store. It would help other
readers discover this book as well.

Thank you in advance!
Jacqui

Words of Wisdom for Teens Series
Award-Winning Guides for Teen Girls

5 Simple Steps to Manage your Mood
A Guide for Teen Girls: How to Let Go of Negative Feelings and Create a Happy Relationship with Yourself and Others

I Would, but MY DAMN MIND Won't Let Me
A Guide for Teen Girls: How to Understand and Control Your Thoughts and Feelings

Jump-Start Your Confidence and Boost Your Self-Esteem
A Guide for Teen Girls: Unleash Your Inner Superpowers to Destroy Fear and Self-Doubt, and Build Unshakable Confidence

Companion Journals

5 Simple Steps to Manage your Mood Journal
A Companion Journal to Help You Track, Understand and Take Charge of Your Mood

I Would, but MY DAMN MIND Won't Let Me
A Companion Journal to Help You Tap into the Power of Your Mind to Be Positive, Happy, and Confident.
Pre-order now on Amazon

Jump-Start Your Confidence and Boost Your Self-Esteem
A Companion Journal to Help You Create a Positive and Powerful Mindset to Conquer Anxiety, Fear, and Self-Doubt
Pre-order now on Amazon

Stop the Bully Within Podcast

After seeing thousands of clients, I noticed a common theme among most of those I help—they are their own biggest bully.

Just pause for a moment and think of the words you say to yourself when you did something wrong or failed at something. Are those loving and supportive words? Would you say those same words to someone you love?

For many people, when they think of a bully, they think of someone outside of them—someone who says and does mean things to cause others pain. Not too many people think about the bully they have within themselves.

I'm on a mission to bring awareness to how damaging this "bully within" can be, and to help people learn how to transform that inner critic into their best friend, cheerleader, and personal champion for success.

Listen to the Podcast at
https://www.jacquiletran.com/podcast